Stellar Sativas and Cosmic Indicas

Stellar Sativas and Cosmic Indicas

Matthew Petchinsky

Apophis Enterprises LLC

<u>Stellar Sativas and Cosmic Indicas</u>
By: Matthew Petchinsky

Chapter 1: Introduction to the Cosmos of Cannabis

In the vast expanse of human culture and scientific inquiry, few plants have sparked as much fascination, controversy, and debate as cannabis. This introductory chapter aims to unravel the intricate tapestry that constitutes the cosmos of cannabis, embarking on a journey that stretches from its ancient origins to its current status in the sphere of legality and societal acceptance. We will explore the dichotomy between Sativa and Indica strains, debunking common myths and shedding light on their unique characteristics. Furthermore, this exploration sets the groundwork for the book's broader ambition: to delve into the scientific intricacies and cultural nuances of cannabis, navigating through its impacts, uses, and evolving significance in contemporary society.

Overview of Cannabis: A Journey Through Time

Cannabis's history is as rich and diverse as its genetic makeup. Archaeological evidence suggests its use dates back over 12,000 years, making it one of humanity's oldest cultivated crops. Initially, it was valued for its fibers, used in making textiles and ropes, and its seeds, consumed for their nutritional value. However, its psychoactive properties did not remain unnoticed, weaving cannabis into the fabric of various ancient cultures.

In ancient China, cannabis was regarded as a medicinal herb, documented in the world's oldest pharmacopeia, the Pen Ts'ao Ching, for its efficacy in treating ailments such as malaria and rheumatism. Its journey westward saw cannabis embraced by ancient Egyptians, Greeks, and

Romans for its healing properties and as an aid in religious ceremonies. Despite its widespread use, the plant's psychoactive effects often placed it at the center of moral and ethical debates throughout history.

The modern era of cannabis began with its global spread during the colonial period, eventually leading to widespread prohibition in the 20th century due to rising concerns over addiction and moral decay. However, the late 20th and early 21st centuries have seen a dramatic shift, with many countries re-evaluating cannabis's legal status, recognizing its medicinal benefits, and, in some regions, decriminalizing or legalizing its recreational use.

Sativa vs. Indica: Understanding the Dichotomy

At the heart of the cannabis cosmos are two primary types: Sativa and Indica. These classifications, which have been both revered and misunderstood, serve as a basic framework for understanding the complex world of cannabis genetics.

Sativa

Cannabis Sativa plants are typically tall, with narrow leaves, and thrive in warm climates. They are known for their uplifting and energizing effects, often enhancing creativity and focus. Sativas are usually recommended for daytime use due to their stimulating properties.

Indica

In contrast, Cannabis Indica plants are shorter, bushier, and have broader leaves. They flourish in cooler climates and are celebrated for their relaxing and sedative effects. Indicas are often preferred for evening use, as they can help with relaxation and sleep.

Common Misconceptions

The Sativa/Indica classification, while useful, is an oversimplification. Modern research suggests that the effects of cannabis are more accurately attributed to the specific chemical composition of the plant, including cannabinoids like THC and CBD, and terpenes, which contribute to its aroma and effects. This understanding challenges the traditional dichotomy, highlighting the need for a more nuanced approach to classifying cannabis.

The Scope of the Book

This book endeavors to bridge the gap between cannabis's storied past and its dynamic present. We aim to dissect the scientific underpinnings that make cannabis a subject of endless fascination, from its pharmacological impacts to the genetic diversity that gives rise to its myriad strains and effects. Concurrently, we will traverse the cultural landscape that cannabis occupies, exploring its role in art, music, medicine, and social movements.

In navigating the cosmos of cannabis, our goal is not only to inform but also to illuminate the complexities and contradictions that surround this enigmatic plant. By embracing both the scientific and cultural dimensions of cannabis, we hope to provide a comprehensive and engaging exploration that resonates with novices and connoisseurs alike.

As we embark on this journey through the stellar sativas and cosmic indicas, we invite you to keep an open mind, challenge preconceived notions, and join us in a quest for understanding that transcends the surface level. Welcome to the cosmos of cannabis, a realm where science and culture intertwine in the most fascinating ways.

If you want to see some amazing products, please visit my Virtual Dispensary: https://shift.store/sg1fan23477/retail

Chapter 2: The Galactic Garden - Understanding Sativas

In the grand cosmos of cannabis, Sativas shine brightly, offering energizing effects and inspiring creativity across the globe. This chapter voyages into the heart of Sativa strains, tracing their ancient origins, examining their botanical nuances, celebrating their most stellar strains, and understanding their roles both culturally and medicinally in society.

Origins and History: Tracing Sativa Strains Back to Their Roots

Cannabis Sativa, with its energizing and uplifting effects, has roots that trace back to Eastern Asia. Historical records suggest that these strains were first used and cultivated in ancient times for their seeds and fibers, long before their psychoactive properties were discovered or utilized. Over millennia, as trade routes expanded, Cannabis Sativa made its way across continents, adapting to various climates and cultures, and becoming a vital part of traditional medicines and rituals.

The name "Sativa" itself, derived from Latin, meaning "cultivated", hints at the intertwined history of humans and this plant species. Sativas were among the first cannabis strains to be classified in the 18th century, reflecting their long-standing cultivation and utilization by human societies.

Botanical Characteristics: How to Identify Sativa Plants and Their Unique Properties

Cannabis Sativa plants are distinguished by their tall stature, often reaching heights of up to 12 feet in outdoor environments. They possess narrow, light green leaves, a reflection of their adaptation to warm climates. The growth cycle of Sativa strains is longer than that of their Indica counterparts, requiring more light to flourish and mature. This extended growth period contributes to their high THC content and the energetic, cerebral high they are known for.

Sativas are also characterized by their pungent aroma, attributed to a rich profile of terpenes such as limonene and pinene, which are believed to contribute to their mood-enhancing and invigorating effects. These botanical characteristics are not only a guide to identifying Sativa plants but also hint at the complex chemistry that underpins their unique effects on the human body and mind.

Stellar Sativa Strains: A Deep Dive into Famous Sativa Strains, Their Effects, and Uses

Sativa strains are celebrated for their potent effects, enhancing creativity, focus, and energy. Some of the most renowned Sativa strains include:

- **Sour Diesel**: Known for its fast-acting and energizing effect, Sour Diesel is a favorite among those seeking a creative spark or an uplifted mood.
- **Green Crack**: Despite its provocative name, Green Crack offers a tangy, fruity flavor and an invigorating mental buzz that keeps fatigue at bay.
- **Jack Herer**: Named after the famous cannabis activist, Jack Herer is prized for its clear-headed, blissful high, and potential medicinal benefits, including pain relief and mood enhancement.

These strains, among others, are not just popular for recreational use; they also have profound medicinal applications, particularly in treating conditions like depression, chronic fatigue, and attention deficit disorders, showcasing the versatile power of Sativa cannabis.

Sativa in Society: Exploring the Cultural and Medicinal Roles of Sativa Strains Across Different Societies

Sativa strains have played a multifaceted role in societies around the world. Culturally, they have been integral to artistic communities, credited with inspiring musicians, writers, and artists with their cerebral high. Sativas have fueled creativity and innovation, contributing to the birth of myriad artworks, music, and literature.

Medicinally, the uplifting and energizing effects of Sativas have been harnessed to combat depression, anxiety, and stress-related disorders. Their ability to enhance focus and energy makes them a valuable tool in treating ADHD and fatigue. The therapeutic potential of Sativas extends into the realm of pain management, where their psychoactive properties can offer relief from chronic pain and migraines.

As our understanding of cannabis deepens, the appreciation for Sativa strains and their contribution to both cultural and medicinal landscapes continues to grow. Their adaptability and the diversity of effects have made Sativas a cornerstone of the cannabis community, illuminating the path towards a more nuanced and holistic understanding of this ancient plant.

In the galactic garden of cannabis, Sativas stand tall, a testament to the enduring relationship between humanity and this versatile plant. As we continue to explore the cosmos of cannabis, the journey through the world of Sativas offers a glimpse into the potential for innovation, healing, and understanding that lies within this celestial plant family.

If you want to see some amazing products, please visit my Virtual Dispensary: https://shift.store/sg1fan23477/retail

Chapter 3: The Nebulous Netherworld of Indicas

In the cosmic dance of the cannabis universe, Indica strains offer a grounding contrast to the energetic twirl of Sativas. These strains draw us into the nebulous netherworld of relaxation, introspection, and healing. This chapter delves into the origins and evolution of Cannabis Indica, outlines its distinctive botanical features, celebrates its most influential strains, and explores its profound impact on culture, art, and wellness practices across the globe.

Origins and History: The Ancient Beginnings of Indica Strains

Cannabis Indica traces its roots back to the rugged landscapes of Central Asia, specifically the regions encompassing the Hindu Kush mountain range. The term "Indica" was first coined in the 18th century to describe the psychoactive varieties of cannabis discovered in India, where they were harvested for their seeds, fiber, and hashish production. Unlike Sativas, Indicas evolved in harsh, variable climates, leading to their distinct morphology and chemical makeup. These plants have been used in traditional Ayurvedic and Middle Eastern medicine for centuries, prized for their sedative and therapeutic properties.

Botanical Characteristics: Identifying Features of Indica Plants

Cannabis Indica plants are typically shorter and bushier than their Sativa counterparts, with dense branches and broad, dark green leaves. They adapt well to cooler climates, featuring a faster flowering cycle that makes them suitable for cultivation in a wide range of environments. The buds of Indica strains are generally thick and resinous, indicative of high cannabinoid concentrations, particularly THC and CBD. This rich cannabinoid profile contributes to the profound physical effects Indicas are known for, including deep relaxation and pain relief.

Botanically, Indicas are distinguished by their pungent aroma, which can vary from sweet and fruity to earthy and skunky. This is due to their terpene profile, which not only influences their scent and flavor but also plays a role in the therapeutic effects attributed to these strains.

Cosmic Indica Strains: Examination of Key Indica Strains, Their Effects, and Therapeutic Benefits

Several Indica strains have risen to prominence for their potent effects and therapeutic potential. Among these cosmic varieties are:

- **Northern Lights**: One of the most famous Indica strains, Northern Lights is celebrated for its ability to relax the body and mind, ease pain, and encourage sleep. Its soothing effects make it a staple for those seeking respite from insomnia and stress.
- **Granddaddy Purple**: Known for its distinct berry aroma and deep purple buds, Granddaddy Purple delivers a blend of cerebral euphoria and physical relaxation. It's widely used for pain relief, muscle relaxation, and combating anxiety.
- **Afghan Kush**: Originating from the Hindu Kush mountain range, Afghan Kush is revered for its heavy resin content and sedative effects, making it ideal for hash production and medicinal use in treating chronic pain and insomnia.

These strains, among others, underscore the therapeutic diversity within Indicas, offering relief from various physical and mental ailments, from chronic pain to anxiety and sleep disorders.

Indica's Cultural Impact: How Indica Strains Have Influenced Music, Art, and Relaxation Practices

Indica strains have woven their way into the fabric of various cultural practices, influencing music, art, and relaxation techniques. In the realm of music, genres such as reggae, hip-hop, and blues have embraced the deep, introspective calm offered by Indicas, often citing them as a source of creative inspiration and spiritual solace. Artists across mediums have turned to Indicas to deepen their connection to their work, finding in these strains a pathway to inner worlds of creativity.

Moreover, Indicas have played a significant role in the development of wellness practices aimed at relaxation and mindfulness. From yoga studios incorporating cannabis into their sessions to enhance relaxation and focus, to meditation retreats using Indicas to aid in achieving deeper states of calm, the influence of these strains on wellness culture is profound.

In the netherworld of Indicas, we find a universe of relaxation, healing, and introspection. These strains remind us of the balance necessary in our lives and our cultures, offering a counterpoint to the ceaseless activity and energy of the modern world. As we continue to explore the cosmos of cannabis, the journey into the heart of Indica strains reveals the depth and diversity of this ancient plant, inviting us to explore the myriad ways it can enrich and enhance our experience of the world.

If you want to see some amazing products, please visit my Virtual Dispensary: https://shift.store/sg1fan23477/retail

Chapter 4: Hybrid Horizons

In the evolving universe of cannabis, hybrid strains represent the frontier of innovation, blending the cosmic qualities of Sativas and the nebulous characteristics of Indicas to create a galaxy of nuanced effects and applications. This chapter delves into the science behind hybridization, explores the stars of the hybrid universe with profiles of notable strains, and examines the pivotal role hybrids play in the dynamic cannabis ecosystem.

The Science of Hybridization: Understanding How and Why Hybrids Are Created

Hybridization in cannabis is the deliberate cross-breeding of Sativa and Indica strains, aiming to combine desirable traits from each into a single plant. This process allows breeders to enhance certain characteristics, such as potency, flavor, yield, and resistance to pests and diseases. The ultimate goal is to produce strains that can offer a balanced high, address specific medical conditions more effectively, or simply provide a new cannabis experience.

Hybrids are often categorized into three types: Sativa-dominant, Indica-dominant, and balanced (50/50). Sativa-dominant hybrids may offer a more cerebral, energizing effect with some physical relaxation, while Indica-dominant hybrids typically provide significant body relaxation with some mental clarity. Balanced hybrids strive to offer an even mix of both Sativa and Indica effects, suitable for those seeking a harmonious experience.

Navigating the Hybrid Universe: Profiles of Notable Hybrid Strains, Their Lineage, and Effects

The hybrid universe is vast and varied, with each strain offering a unique journey. Some of the most notable hybrid strains include:

- **Blue Dream**: A Sativa-dominant hybrid beloved for its soothing cerebral high and gentle body relaxation. Originating from a cross between Blueberry (Indica) and Haze (Sativa), Blue Dream is popular for its sweet berry aroma and balanced effects, making it suitable for treating symptoms of stress, depression, and pain.
- **GSC (Girl Scout Cookies)**: This Indica-dominant hybrid, stemming from a blend of OG Kush and Durban Poison, is renowned for its potent effects that offer a euphoric high and deep relaxation. Its sweet and earthy flavors have made it a favorite among connoisseurs for treating pain, nausea, and appetite loss.
- **GG4 (Gorilla Glue #4)**: A balanced hybrid known for its heavy-handed euphoria and relaxation, GG4 comes from a lineage that includes Chem's Sister, Sour Dubb, and Chocolate Diesel. This strain delivers a pungent aroma and is sought after for its ability to relieve stress, pain, and insomnia.

These profiles represent just a glimpse into the hybrid universe, where each strain is a star with its own story, effects, and therapeutic potential.

Hybrids in the Cannabis Ecosystem: The Role of Hybrids in Evolving Cannabis Culture and Consumption

Hybrids play a critical role in the cannabis ecosystem, driving innovation in cultivation, consumption, and cultural acceptance. They have expanded the palette of effects, flavors, and aromas available to consumers, allowing for a more personalized cannabis experience. Hybrids meet the diverse needs and preferences of a broad audience, from recreational users seeking unique highs to medical patients needing specific symptom relief.

The creation of hybrids has also fostered a deeper appreciation and understanding of cannabis genetics and the potential for targeted effects. This has led to a more sophisticated cannabis culture, where enthusiasts discuss and seek out strains based on their specific cannabinoid and terpene profiles, rather than simply choosing between Sativa and Indica.

Furthermore, hybrids have been at the forefront of the push for legal cannabis reform, showcasing the plant's versatility and its potential for therapeutic use. As cannabis continues to move into the mainstream, hybrids will undoubtedly play a pivotal role in shaping the future of cannabis culture and consumption, navigating the ever-expanding universe of possibilities.

In the horizon of hybrids, we discover not just the blending of Sativa and Indica genetics, but the merging of past and future, tradition and innovation, offering a glimpse into the boundless potential of the cannabis cosmos. As we journey through the hybrid universe, we are reminded of the endless possibilities that arise from exploration, creativity, and a deep respect for this remarkable plant.

If you want to see some amazing products, please visit my Virtual Dispensary: https://shift.store/sg1fan23477/retail

Chapter 5: Cannabinoids and Terpenes - The Molecular Makeup

Within the stellar expanse of the cannabis cosmos, the true magic resides at the molecular level, where cannabinoids and terpenes orchestrate a symphony of effects, flavors, and aromas. This chapter ventures beyond the well-trodden paths of THC and CBD to explore the vast array of cannabinoids that define the unique characteristics of cannabis strains. It delves into the world of terpenes, the aromatic architects of the cannabis plant, and unpacks the science behind the entourage effect, where these compounds work in concert to amplify the therapeutic potential of cannabis.

Beyond THC and CBD: A Look into the Wide Array of Cannabinoids

While THC (tetrahydrocannabinol) and CBD (cannabidiol) are the most renowned cannabinoids for their psychoactive and therapeutic effects, respectively, they are but two stars in a galaxy of over a hundred known cannabinoids. Each of these compounds contributes to the plant's effects, and understanding their roles offers insight into the nuanced experiences cannabis can provide.

- **CBN (Cannabinol):** Known for its sedative properties, CBN is a byproduct of THC degradation. It is often sought after for its potential to treat insomnia and relieve pain.
- **CBG (Cannabigerol):** Referred to as the "mother of all cannabinoids," CBG is a precursor from which other cannabinoids are synthesized. It shows promise in treating glaucoma, inflammatory bowel disease, and even certain cancers.
- **THCV (Tetrahydrocannabivarin):** Similar in molecular structure to THC, THCV offers a unique array of effects, including appetite suppression, which contrasts the typical hunger-inducing properties of THC. It also shows potential in regulating blood sugar levels and reducing panic attacks.

This exploration into the broader spectrum of cannabinoids reveals the potential for targeted therapies and customized cannabis experiences, highlighting the plant's complex chemistry and its myriad applications.

The Aromatic Architects: Understanding Terpenes and Their Influence on Effects and Aromas

Terpenes are the aromatic compounds found in many plants, including cannabis, responsible for their distinct smells and flavors. In cannabis, terpenes do more than just influence the sensory experience; they also affect the plant's effects, interacting with cannabinoids to produce varied and nuanced experiences.

- **Myrcene**: The most abundant terpene in cannabis, myrcene, is known for its earthy, musky notes. It is believed to enhance THC's psychoactive effects and contribute to the sedative quality of many Indica strains.
- **Limonene**: With its refreshing citrus aroma, limonene is thought to elevate mood and provide stress relief. It also has antifungal and antibacterial properties.
- **Pinene**: True to its name, pinene imparts a pine-like aroma. It's known for its anti-inflammatory effects and ability to improve airflow and respiratory functions.

These terpenes, along with dozens of others, play a pivotal role in the therapeutic and recreational appeal of cannabis, influencing everything from mood and behavior to physiological responses.

The Entourage Effect: How Cannabinoids and Terpenes Work Together to Enhance Cannabis's Effects

The entourage effect is a concept that suggests the therapeutic benefits of cannabis are most profound when its myriad compounds interact synergistically, rather than in isolation. This theory posits that cannabinoids and terpenes enhance each other's effects and mitigate potential side effects, creating a balanced, holistic experience.

Research into the entourage effect is ongoing, but early findings suggest that the interactions between these compounds can lead to enhanced pain relief, reduced inflammation, improved mood, and a host of other benefits. For instance, CBD is believed to counteract some of THC's less desirable effects, such as anxiety and paranoia, while certain terpenes may bolster THC's efficacy or extend the duration of its effects.

Understanding the molecular makeup of cannabis and the interplay between cannabinoids and terpenes opens up new avenues for the customization and optimization of cannabis products, catering to individual needs and preferences. This chapter underscores the complexity and potential of cannabis, inviting further exploration into the molecular universe that underpins the plant's diverse effects.

As we delve deeper into the molecular makeup of cannabis, we uncover the intricate dance of cannabinoids and terpenes, a testament to the plant's evolutionary sophistication and its potential to revolutionize our approach to wellness and recreation. This exploration into the heart of cannabis's molecular world reveals not just the science behind the plant's effects, but the boundless possibilities it holds for enhancing the human experience.

If you want to see some amazing products, please visit my Virtual Dispensary: https://shift.store/sg1fan23477/retail

Chapter 6: Growing the Galaxy - Cultivation Techniques

Cultivating the cosmic garden of cannabis requires a blend of art, science, and a deep understanding of the plant's needs. This chapter explores the divergent cultivation techniques suited to Sativas and Indicas, delves into advanced horticultural innovations that have revolutionized cannabis farming, and underscores the importance of sustainable practices in nurturing our planetary ecosystem. Through mastery of these methods, cultivators can navigate the challenges and rewards of growing the galaxy of cannabis.

Sativa vs. Indica Cultivation: How Growing Techniques Vary by Strain

The cultivation journey diverges significantly between Sativa and Indica strains, each demanding specific conditions to flourish and reveal their stellar qualities.

Sativa Cultivation

Sativas, with their tall stature and lengthy flowering times, are well-suited to outdoor environments where they can bask in ample sunlight. These strains thrive in warm, equatorial climates, requiring a longer vegetative growth phase to reach their full potential. Cultivators often employ training techniques such as topping and super cropping to manage their height and encourage more lateral growth, making them more manageable and increasing yield.

Indica Cultivation

Indicas, in contrast, are compact and bushy, making them ideal for indoor cultivation where space is at a premium. Their shorter flowering time allows for quicker harvests. Indoor environments offer greater control over conditions such as light, temperature, and humidity, which can be optimized for Indicas to enhance their dense flower production. Techniques like Sea of Green (SOG) are popular for maximizing yield in these environments.

Advanced Horticulture: Innovations and Methods in Cannabis Cultivation

The field of cannabis cultivation has seen remarkable innovations, driven by the desire to enhance efficiency, yield, and quality. Some of these advancements include:

- **Hydroponics**: This soilless cultivation method uses nutrient-rich water to grow cannabis, allowing for faster growth and greater yield. Hydroponics systems can be highly efficient, conserving water and nutrients by recirculating them through the system.
- **Aeroponics**: An evolution of hydroponics, aeroponics suspends plants in air, misting their roots with nutrient solution. This method maximizes oxygen exposure to roots, promoting rapid growth and high densities of cultivation.
- **LED Lighting**: Advances in LED technology have provided cultivators with energy-efficient lighting that emits specific light spectra to optimize growth and flowering, reducing electricity consumption and heat generation compared to traditional HID lamps.

Sustainability in Space: Eco-friendly and Sustainable Growing Practices

As cannabis cultivation scales up, its environmental footprint becomes a critical consideration. Sustainable cultivation practices are vital in minimizing this impact, ensuring that the galaxy of cannabis grows in harmony with our planet.

- **Organic Cultivation**: Using organic nutrients and pest management strategies reduces the chemical runoff and soil degradation associated with conventional farming, preserving local ecosystems.
- **Water Conservation**: Techniques such as drip irrigation and the capture and reuse of water in hydroponic and aeroponic systems

significantly reduce water use, a crucial consideration in drought-prone areas.

- **Renewable Energy**: Powering cultivation operations with renewable energy sources like solar or wind reduces greenhouse gas emissions, mitigating climate change impact.

Cultivating cannabis, whether on a personal scale or commercially, demands not just a commitment to the plant but also to the environment that sustains it. By adopting advanced cultivation techniques and prioritizing sustainability, growers can contribute to a future where the cannabis industry thrives as a model of responsible agricultural practice.

In navigating the cultivation of the cannabis galaxy, we uncover the delicate balance between innovation and tradition, science and nature. This journey through the varied landscapes of Sativa and Indica cultivation, advanced horticultural methods, and sustainable practices offers a blueprint for growing not just cannabis, but a healthier, greener world.

If you want to see some amazing products, please visit my Virtual Dispensary: https://shift.store/sg1fan23477/retail

Chapter 7: Medicinal Moons - Health and Healing

As we voyage through the cosmos of cannabis, the medicinal moons orbiting this complex galaxy offer a realm of profound healing and therapeutic potential. This chapter delves into the historical and contemporary uses of cannabis in medicine, explores the therapeutic benefits of Indica, Sativa, and hybrid strains for various ailments, and gazes into the future of cannabis in healthcare, illuminating the path of potential developments and research frontiers.

Cannabis in Medicine: Historical and Contemporary Medicinal Uses of Cannabis

Cannabis's journey as a medicinal herb spans thousands of years, with ancient civilizations recognizing its healing properties. From the ancient Chinese using it to alleviate pain and treat various conditions, to its inclusion in the pharmacopeias of medieval Islamic scholars for its anti-inflammatory and analgesic effects, cannabis has been a cornerstone of traditional medicine across cultures.

In contemporary medicine, the resurgence of interest in cannabis's therapeutic potential has led to its recognition as a valuable tool in treating a wide range of conditions. The discovery of the endocannabinoid system (ECS) in the late 20th century provided a scientific foundation for understanding how cannabis interacts with the human body to exert its effects. Today, medical cannabis is used to manage chronic pain, reduce nausea from chemotherapy, treat wasting syndrome in HIV/AIDS patients, and alleviate symptoms of neurological disorders like multiple sclerosis and epilepsy.

Indica, Sativa, and Hybrids for Health: Which Strains Help What Ailments

The therapeutic application of cannabis strains is as varied as the conditions they aim to treat, with Indica, Sativa, and hybrid strains each offering unique benefits.

- **Indica Strains** are often sought for their relaxing and sedative effects, making them suitable for treating insomnia, anxiety, and muscle spasms. Their body-focused effects also make Indicas a good choice for managing chronic pain and reducing inflammation.
- **Sativa Strains** are characterized by their uplifting and energizing effects, which can be beneficial for addressing fatigue, depression, and attention deficit disorders. Sativas may also enhance creativity and focus, offering a cerebral reprieve from mental health conditions.
- **Hybrid Strains** combine the traits of Indicas and Sativas, allowing patients to tailor their treatment to specific needs. For instance, a Sativa-dominant hybrid might be perfect for someone seeking pain relief without sedation, while an Indica-dominant hybrid could be ideal for someone needing to alleviate anxiety while also managing pain.

The Future of Cannabis in Healthcare: Potential Developments and Research Frontiers

The future of cannabis in healthcare is as expansive as the universe itself, with ongoing research poised to unlock further therapeutic potentials of this ancient plant. The following areas represent key frontiers in the medicinal exploration of cannabis:

- **Personalized Medicine**: Advances in genetics and pharmacology could enable tailored cannabis treatments that are optimized for an individual's genetic makeup, improving efficacy and reducing side effects.
- **Cannabinoid and Terpene Synergy**: Deeper understanding of the entourage effect and how cannabinoids and terpenes interact could lead to the development of highly specialized strain profiles for specific conditions.

- **Non-Psychoactive Cannabinoids**: Research into cannabinoids like CBDV (cannabidivarin) and THCV (tetrahydrocannabivarin) offers the potential for treatments that harness the therapeutic benefits of cannabis without psychoactive effects, expanding its applicability in medicine.
- **Clinical Trials and Regulation**: As the legal landscape around cannabis continues to evolve, increased research and clinical trials will provide the robust evidence needed to integrate cannabis more fully into mainstream medicine, potentially leading to new drug developments and treatment protocols.

In navigating the medicinal moons of cannabis, we uncover a world rich with potential for healing and discovery. As research and understanding deepen, the role of cannabis in healthcare continues to evolve, promising a future where its full therapeutic spectrum is realized and integrated into holistic health practices, illuminating new paths to wellness and healing in the cosmic garden of cannabis.

If you want to see some amazing products, please visit my Virtual Dispensary: https://shift.store/sg1fan23477/retail

Chapter 8: Legal Landscapes - Navigating Through Nebulas

In the celestial journey of cannabis, navigating through the legal landscapes presents a challenge akin to traversing nebulous galaxies. This chapter delves into the complex legal status of cannabis across the globe, examines the profound impact legislation has had on its cultivation, sale, and use, and highlights the ongoing advocacy efforts pushing for legalization and regulation. This exploration offers insights into the shifting paradigms and future legal frontiers of cannabis.

A World of Laws: The Complex Legal Status of Cannabis Globally

The global legal landscape of cannabis is a patchwork quilt of policies and attitudes, varying significantly from one country to another and even within regions of the same country. In some parts of the world, cannabis is celebrated and integrated into society, while in others, it remains ensnared in legal restrictions.

- **Legalization and Decriminalization**: Nations like Canada, Uruguay, and several U.S. states have taken progressive steps by legalizing cannabis for recreational and medicinal use, setting up regulated markets to control its production and sale. Others have opted for decriminalization, reducing penalties associated with cannabis possession and use, aiming to curb the impacts of drug-related criminal charges on individuals and society.

- **Medicinal Use**: Many countries have recognized the therapeutic benefits of cannabis, legalizing its use for medical purposes. This shift acknowledges the plant's potential in treating a range of conditions, from chronic pain to epilepsy, and opens the door for further research and development.

- **Strict Prohibitions**: Despite a global trend towards legalization and decriminalization, some countries maintain strict anti-cannabis laws, with severe penalties for possession, use, and trafficking. These policies reflect cultural, religious, and political factors that influence national drug laws.

The Impact of Legislation: How Laws Have Shaped the Cultivation, Sale, and Use of Cannabis

The legal frameworks governing cannabis have profoundly influenced its cultivation, sale, and consumption, impacting everything from agricultural practices to economic markets and social behaviors.

- **Cultivation**: Legalization in some regions has led to the emergence of licensed cultivation centers, adopting advanced agricultural technologies and sustainable practices. In contrast, in regions where cannabis remains illegal, cultivation often occurs in hidden or remote locations, sometimes at the expense of environmental conservation.
- **Sale and Distribution**: Legal markets have facilitated the establishment of dispensaries and cannabis shops, providing regulated spaces for the sale of cannabis products. These establishments offer consumers a safe environment to purchase cannabis, ensuring product quality and potency. Conversely, in places where cannabis is illegal, the black market flourishes, eluding regulation and quality control.
- **Use and Social Perception**: Legalization and decriminalization have contributed to changing social perceptions of cannabis, increasingly normalizing its use both medicinally and recreationally. This shift has encouraged open discussions about cannabis, reducing stigma and promoting a more informed understanding of its effects and benefits.

Advocacy and Future Legal Frontiers: Efforts Towards Legalization and Regulation

The path to cannabis legalization and regulation is paved by the tireless efforts of advocates and organizations dedicated to reforming outdated and unjust drug laws. These advocates work to highlight the economic, social, and medical benefits of legalization, pushing for change through:

- **Education and Awareness**: Dispelling myths about cannabis, providing evidence-based information on its benefits and risks, and educating the public and policymakers about the potential advantages of legalization.
- **Policy Reform**: Engaging in legislative processes, supporting cannabis reform bills, and working towards the implementation of fair and effective cannabis laws that prioritize public health and safety.
- **International Cooperation**: Collaborating with international bodies and other countries to share best practices, research findings, and policy successes to support global shifts towards more progressive cannabis policies.

As we navigate the legal landscapes of cannabis, the journey reveals a world in flux, with nations at various stages of embracing the plant's potential. The ongoing advocacy and push for legal reform envision a future where cannabis is recognized and regulated as a valuable resource, offering benefits that span medicinal, economic, and social realms. In navigating through these nebulous legal terrains, the goal remains clear: to establish a global framework that acknowledges cannabis's complexity, respects individual freedoms, and harnesses its potential for the greater good.

If you want to see some amazing products, please visit my Virtual Dispensary: https://shift.store/sg1fan23477/retail

Chapter 9: Cosmic Culture - Cannabis in Society

As we journey deeper into the cosmos of cannabis, we discover its profound influence on human culture, weaving through the fabric of creativity, social interaction, and ritualistic practices. This chapter explores the symbiotic relationship between cannabis and artistic endeavors, examines how different strains facilitate unique social experiences, and delves into the ceremonial use of cannabis across various cultures, highlighting its integral role in society's cosmic tapestry.

Cannabis and Creativity: Exploring the Connection Between Cannabis and Artistic Endeavors

The nexus between cannabis and creativity has long captivated artists, writers, musicians, and creators across the spectrum of cultural production. This relationship is rooted in the way cannabis interacts with the mind, often enhancing sensory perception, breaking down conventional thought barriers, and facilitating novel connections.

- **Music and Literature**: From the jazz musicians of the Harlem Renaissance to the beat poets and beyond, cannabis has been credited with opening channels of creativity, allowing artists to explore and express complex emotions and thoughts through their work.
- **Visual Arts**: Many visual artists use cannabis to enhance their perception of colors and forms, diving deeper into the abstract and surreal, and capturing their visions in unique and compelling ways.
- **Creative Problem-Solving**: Beyond the arts, cannabis is recognized for its ability to aid in creative problem-solving, enabling individuals to approach challenges from new perspectives in fields as diverse as technology, science, and entrepreneurship.

Social Sativas and Indicas: How Different Strains Facilitate Social Interactions and Solitude

Cannabis's influence extends beyond the individual, shaping social interactions and experiences. The effects of Sativa and Indica strains can either catalyze communal connection or deepen personal introspection.

- **Sativas for Socializing**: Sativa strains are often associated with uplifting and energizing effects, making them popular choices for social gatherings and activities. They can stimulate conversation, laughter, and a shared sense of euphoria, enhancing the communal experience.
- **Indicas for Introspection**: In contrast, Indica strains tend to promote relaxation and introspection, ideal for solitary reflection or intimate gatherings. The calming effect of Indicas can facilitate a deeper connection with oneself or close companions, fostering a sense of peace and contentment.
- **Hybrids for Harmony**: Hybrid strains offer a balance, providing flexibility for either social or solitary experiences based on their dominant characteristics. This versatility makes hybrids particularly appealing for those seeking to tailor their cannabis experience to specific social settings or moods.

Rituals and Recreation: The Ceremonial Use of Cannabis in Various Cultures

The use of cannabis in rituals and ceremonies is a testament to its deep roots in human culture, serving as a bridge between the physical and spiritual worlds across civilizations.

- **Ancient Ceremonies**: Historical records from ancient China, India, and the Middle East document the use of cannabis in religious and spiritual rituals, where it was used to facilitate meditation, healing, and communion with the divine.

- **Indigenous Practices**: Many indigenous cultures have used cannabis in their ceremonial practices for centuries, recognizing its power to heal, protect, and connect with ancestral spirits.
- **Modern Spirituality**: In contemporary society, the ritualistic use of cannabis continues to evolve, with new-age movements and spiritual practices incorporating cannabis as a tool for meditation, mindfulness, and personal growth.

Cannabis's role in society transcends its physical properties, embedding itself in the cultural DNA of humanity. Its ability to inspire creativity, shape social experiences, and connect us to deeper spiritual truths underscores its significance in the cosmic culture. As we explore the societal dimensions of cannabis, we uncover a multifaceted relationship that reflects the complexity of human experience, offering insights into the past, present, and future of this enigmatic plant within the tapestry of human culture.

If you want to see some amazing products, please visit my Virtual Dispensary: https://shift.store/sg1fan23477/retail

Chapter 10: The Future Frontiers of Cannabis

As we reach the outer limits of our exploration into the cosmos of cannabis, we stand on the precipice of new and uncharted territories. The future of cannabis is illuminated by technological innovations, the tantalizing potential of astro-botanical endeavors, and the evolving societal and cultural integration of this ancient plant. This final chapter peers into the horizon, envisioning the transformative possibilities that lie ahead in the ongoing journey of cannabis through human civilization.

Technological Innovations: The Role of Technology in Advancing Cannabis Cultivation and Consumption

The intersection of technology and cannabis has catalyzed a renaissance in cultivation methods, consumption devices, and product innovation, setting the stage for a future where technology continues to revolutionize our relationship with this plant.

- **Cultivation Technologies**: Advanced LED lighting, automated hydroponic and aeroponic systems, and precision agriculture techniques are pushing the boundaries of efficiency, sustainability, and quality in cannabis cultivation. Genetic sequencing and CRISPR technology hold the promise of unlocking new cannabis strains with tailored cannabinoid and terpene profiles, optimizing both medical efficacy and recreational experience.
- **Consumption Devices**: Innovations in vaporization technology, nanoemulsification, and controlled-dose edibles are transforming the way cannabis is consumed, offering safer, cleaner, and more controlled experiences. The integration of smart technology with cannabis devices, such as app-controlled vaporizers, provides users with unprecedented control over their consumption.

- **Blockchain and Cannabis**: The application of blockchain technology in the cannabis industry promises enhanced transparency and traceability, from seed to sale. This could improve regulatory compliance, product quality assurance, and consumer trust in a market that values authenticity and safety.

Space Strains: The Potential for Growing Cannabis in Space and Future Astro-Botanical Endeavors

The final frontier for cannabis cultivation may well be outer space. The unique conditions of microgravity environments offer fascinating possibilities for studying cannabis growth and development, potentially leading to breakthroughs in our understanding of plant biology.

- **Astro-Botanical Research**: Initial forays into growing plants in space, such as experiments aboard the International Space Station, hint at the potential for cannabis cultivation in extraterrestrial environments. Research in these conditions can reveal how variables like gravity and radiation impact plant growth, stress responses, and cannabinoid production.
- **Space Strains**: The prospect of developing cannabis strains specifically adapted for growth in space presents an intriguing avenue for future research. These "space strains" could exhibit unique characteristics or enhanced qualities, driven by the stressors and stimuli of off-Earth environments.

Global Ganja: Predictions for the Future Societal Integration and Cultural Evolution of Cannabis

As legal barriers continue to fall and societal perceptions shift, the future of cannabis in society promises greater integration and cultural evolution.

- **Normalization and Mainstream Acceptance**: The continued trend toward legalization and decriminalization globally is likely to bring cannabis more fully into the mainstream. This will foster a cultural shift towards viewing cannabis as a normal part of everyday life, akin to alcohol or caffeine.

- **Medicinal Breakthroughs**: Ongoing research and clinical trials are set to unlock further medicinal uses of cannabis, potentially leading to its integration into conventional medical treatments and health and wellness industries.
- **Cultural Renaissance**: As cannabis becomes further embedded in social fabric, we can expect a renaissance of sorts in arts, literature, and entertainment, where cannabis-inspired creativity and experiences bloom.
- **Global Cannabis Economy**: The burgeoning global cannabis market will continue to evolve, with innovations in products, services, and experiences driving economic growth, job creation, and international trade in cannabis-related goods.

As we gaze into the future frontiers of cannabis, we see a landscape ripe with potential for growth, discovery, and transformation. The journey of cannabis, from ancient times to its stellar future, mirrors humanity's own quest for knowledge, well-being, and connection. In embracing the possibilities that lie ahead, we embark on a continued exploration of this remarkable plant, uncovering new horizons in the cosmic garden of cannabis.

If you want to see some amazing products, please visit my Virtual Dispensary: https://shift.store/sg1fan23477/retail

Epilogue: The Endless Universe of Cannabis

As our odyssey through the cosmos of cannabis draws to a close, we find ourselves at the threshold of infinite possibilities. The universe of cannabis, with its celestial bodies of science, culture, law, and innovation, stretches out before us, a boundless frontier awaiting further exploration. This journey has taken us from the ancient roots of cannabis in the cradle of civilization to the cutting-edge of technological advancements, from the inner sanctum of personal experience to the global stage of cultural and legal evolution.

Reflecting on the Journey: Summarizing the Expansive World of Cannabis Explored in the Book

We began our voyage by charting the history and types of cannabis, understanding the foundational strains of Sativa and Indica, and the myriad hybrids that blend the two. We delved into the scientific wonders of cannabinoids and terpenes, unraveling the molecular makeup that bestows cannabis with its therapeutic and psychoactive powers. Our exploration took us through the gardens of cultivation, revealing the art and science that nourish the growth of this remarkable plant.

We ventured into the realms of medicinal moons, where cannabis serves as a beacon of healing and hope for many, offering relief and comfort from a constellation of ailments. The legal landscapes revealed the challenges and triumphs of cannabis legislation, marking the path of progress through the nebula of global policies. In the cosmic culture of cannabis, we celebrated the plant's profound influence on creativity, social interaction, and ritualistic practice, highlighting its integral role in human society.

A Call to Exploration: Encouraging Readers to Continue Learning and Engaging with the Cannabis Community

The journey through the cosmos of cannabis does not end here; it merely transitions to a new phase of discovery and understanding. The universe of cannabis is ever-expanding, with new research, strains, technologies, and cultural shifts continuously reshaping our relationship with this ancient plant. As explorers of this universe, we are all part of a community of learners, advocates, and enthusiasts, united in our curiosity and passion for cannabis.

I encourage you, dear reader, to continue your exploration of the cannabis cosmos. Engage with the vibrant community of cultivators, researchers, medical professionals, legal experts, and fellow enthusiasts. Stay informed about the latest developments in cannabis science, legislation, and culture. Experiment responsibly with the myriad strains and products available, always mindful of the laws and regulations in your corner of the galaxy.

Most importantly, share your knowledge and experiences with others. The universe of cannabis is enriched by the diversity of its explorers, and every story, insight, and discovery contributes to our collective understanding of this remarkable plant.

As we conclude this cosmic journey, let us carry forward the spirit of exploration, openness, and respect that defines the cannabis community. The endless universe of cannabis awaits, filled with mysteries to unravel, challenges to overcome, and wonders to behold. Together, let us continue to navigate this universe, guided by the stars of science, compassion, and curiosity, towards a future where the full potential of cannabis is realized for the betterment of all.

If you want to see some amazing products, please visit my Virtual Dispensary: https://shift.store/sg1fan23477/retail

-

-

-

-

-

Appendices for Stellar Sativas and Cosmic Indicas
Appendix A: Cannabis Glossary

This glossary serves as a comprehensive guide to the terminology associated with cannabis culture, science, and law. It is designed to demystify the complex language surrounding cannabis, making the world of cannabis more accessible to enthusiasts, patients, researchers, and the general public.

A

- **Anandamide**: An endocannabinoid produced naturally in the body that binds to cannabinoid receptors, influencing bodily functions such as appetite, memory, and pain.
- **Autoflowering**: A type of cannabis plant that automatically transitions from the vegetative stage to the flowering stage with age, rather than in response to light cycle changes.

B

- **BHO (Butane Hash Oil)**: A potent concentrate of cannabinoids made by dissolving cannabis in butane. Known for its high THC content.
- **Bud**: The flower of the cannabis plant, harvested for medicinal or recreational use due to its concentration of cannabinoids and terpenes.

C

- **CBD (Cannabidiol)**: A non-psychoactive cannabinoid known for its potential therapeutic effects, including reducing inflammation and anxiety.
- **CBG (Cannabigerol)**: A non-psychoactive cannabinoid, often referred to as the "mother of all cannabinoids," because other cannabinoids are derived from its acid form, CBGA.
- **Cannabinoids**: Chemical compounds found in cannabis that interact with the body's endocannabinoid system to produce various effects.
- **Cannabis**: A genus of flowering plants in the family Cannabaceae, which includes species commonly known as marijuana and hemp.
- **Concentrates**: Highly potent substances made by extracting cannabinoids and terpenes from the cannabis plant. Examples include hash, wax, and oils.

D

- **Decarboxylation**: A process that activates cannabinoids in cannabis through heat, making them available for absorption by the body.
- **Dabbing**: A method of consuming cannabis concentrates by vaporizing them on a hot surface and inhaling the vapor.

E

- **Edibles**: Food products infused with cannabis extracts, consumed for medicinal or recreational effects.
- **Endocannabinoid System (ECS)**: A complex cell-signaling system identified in the 1990s that plays a role in regulating a range of functions and processes, including sleep, mood, appetite, and memory.

F

- **Feminized Seeds**: Cannabis seeds that have been bred to produce female plants exclusively, ensuring that all plants will produce buds.

H

- **Hemp**: A variety of Cannabis sativa plant species grown primarily for the industrial uses of its derived products. It is low in THC and can be used to make a variety of products including textiles, biofuel, and health foods.

I

- **Indica**: A species or variety of cannabis known for producing a body high, typically used for its relaxing and sedative effects.

M

- **Microdosing**: The practice of consuming small, sub-psychoactive doses of cannabis to achieve the desired medical benefits without experiencing a significant alteration in mood or perception.

P

- **Phenotype**: The set of observable characteristics of a cannabis plant resulting from the interaction of its genetic makeup with the environment.
- **Psychoactive**: Substances that change brain function and result in alterations in perception, mood, consciousness, cognition, or behavior.

R

- **Rosin**: A solventless cannabis concentrate made by applying heat and pressure to cannabis flowers or kief, resulting in the extraction of the resin.

S

- **Sativa**: A species or variety of cannabis known for producing a cerebral, energizing high, often used for its uplifting effects.
- **Strain**: A specific variety of cannabis plant, bred for certain characteristics like flavor, aroma, effect, and yield.
- **Synthetic Cannabinoids**: Man-made chemicals designed to mimic the effects of natural cannabinoids, often with much stronger and unpredictable effects.

T

- **Terpenes**: Aromatic compounds found in many plants, including cannabis, responsible for the plant's fragrance and flavor. Terpenes may also influence the effects of cannabis by modulating the activity of cannabinoids.
- **THC (Tetrahydrocannabinol)**: The main psychoactive compound in cannabis, responsible for the high sensation.
- **Tincture**: A cannabis-infused liquid solution, often alcohol-based, consumed orally or sublingually (under the tongue).

V

- **Vaporizer**: A device used to consume cannabis by heating the flower or concentrate to a temperature that vaporizes, but does not burn, the cannabinoids and terpenes, producing a vapor to be inhaled.

This glossary is intended as a starting point for those seeking to deepen their understanding of cannabis and its multifaceted role in culture, science, and law. As the cannabis landscape continues to evolve, so too will the language we use to describe and navigate it.

Appendix B: Cannabis Strain Directory

This directory serves as a comprehensive guide to some of the most notable cannabis strains across the Sativa, Indica, and hybrid categories. Each entry highlights the strain's origins, typical effects, and potential medicinal uses, offering a window into the rich diversity within the cannabis species. This resource is designed for educational purposes, to assist enthusiasts, patients, and the curious in navigating the vast universe of cannabis strains.

<u>**Sativa Strains**</u>

1. Sour Diesel

- **Origins**: Believed to have descended from Chemdawg 91 and Super Skunk.
- **Typical Effects**: Energizing, dreamy cerebral effects that have pushed Sour Diesel to its legendary status. Expect a fast-acting invigorating high.
- **Medicinal Uses**: Often used to alleviate depression, pain, and fatigue.

2. Green Crack

- **Origins**: Mythically linked to Snoop Dogg, this strain boasts an energetic and uplifting high. Its lineage is often disputed, though it's generally believed to be a cross between Skunk #1 and an unknown Indica.
- **Typical Effects**: Sharp energy and focus as it induces an invigorating mental buzz.
- **Medicinal Uses**: Ideal for treating fatigue, stress, and depression.

3. Jack Herer

- **Origins**: A tribute to the famed cannabis activist, this strain is a cross between Haze, Northern Lights #5, and Shiva Skunk.
- **Typical Effects**: A blissful, clear-headed, and creative high.
- **Medicinal Uses**: Used for treating low energy, depression, and fatigue.

Indica Strains

1. Northern Lights

- **Origins**: One of the most famous Indicas, its lineage is thought to have originated from indigenous Afghani and Thai landrace strains.
- **Typical Effects**: Comforting euphoria followed by relaxation.
- **Medicinal Uses**: Highly effective for pain relief, stress, and insomnia.

2. Granddaddy Purple

- **Origins**: Created by Ken Estes in 2003, this strain is a well-known Indica cross between Purple Urkle and Big Bud.
- **Typical Effects**: Famous for its dreamy euphoria that blankets the mind in calmness.
- **Medicinal Uses**: Ideal for pain, stress, insomnia, appetite loss, and muscle spasms.

3. Afghan Kush

- **Origins**: Stemming from the Hindu Kush mountain range near the Afghanistan-Pakistan border.
- **Typical Effects**: Deep relaxation and euphoria, presenting a heavy body sensation.

- **Medicinal Uses**: Often sought for its heavy resin content and powerfully sedating effects, useful in treating insomnia, pain, and stress disorders.

Hybrid Strains
1. Blue Dream

- **Origins**: A sativa-dominant hybrid originating in California, has achieved legendary West Coast status. It's a cross between Blueberry indica and sativa Haze.
- **Typical Effects**: Balances full-body relaxation with a gentle cerebral invigoration.
- **Medicinal Uses**: Popular for daytime treatment of symptoms of depression, chronic pain, and nausea.

2. GG4 (Gorilla Glue #4)

- **Origins**: A potent hybrid strain that delivers heavy-handed euphoria and relaxation, leaving you feeling "glued" to the couch. Its origins trace back to Chem's Sister, Sour Dubb, and Chocolate Diesel.
- **Typical Effects**: Heavy sedation and euphoria.
- **Medicinal Uses**: Used for treating pain, stress, and depression.

3. GSC (Girl Scout Cookies)

- **Origins**: An OG Kush and Durban Poison hybrid cross whose reputation grew too large to stay within the borders of its California homeland.
- **Typical Effects**: Offers a euphoric high and strong feelings of relaxation.
- **Medicinal Uses**: Effective at treating anxiety, stress, and depression, appetite loss, and chronic pain.

This directory is not exhaustive but represents a curated selection of strains known for their distinctive effects and medicinal properties. The cannabis landscape is constantly evolving, with new strains and genetics emerging as breeders mix and match genetics to achieve new heights in flavor, potency, and therapeutic efficacy. As you explore these strains, remember that the effects of cannabis can vary widely among individuals, influenced by factors such as tolerance, consumption method, and the plant's cannabinoid and terpene profiles.

Appendix C: Legal Status by Region

The legal status of cannabis varies dramatically around the world, reflecting a complex patchwork of laws and regulations that govern its use, cultivation, possession, and sale. This appendix provides an overview of cannabis legality in various countries and states, highlighting the distinctions between medicinal and recreational use. It's important to note that laws are continually evolving, and while this appendix offers a snapshot of current regulations, always verify the latest legal status in your area.

North America

United States

- **Medicinal Use**: Legal in 33 states, plus the District of Columbia, Guam, Puerto Rico, and the U.S. Virgin Islands.
- **Recreational Use**: Legal in 11 states and the District of Columbia. Note that cannabis remains illegal at the federal level.

Canada

- **Medicinal Use**: Legal nationwide since 2001.
- **Recreational Use**: Legal nationwide since October 17, 2018.

Mexico

- **Medicinal Use**: Legal with restrictions since June 2017.
- **Recreational Use**: Supreme Court decriminalized personal use in a landmark ruling, but comprehensive legislation is pending.

Europe

Netherlands

- **Medicinal Use**: Legal.

- **Recreational Use:** Decriminalized; sale and consumption allowed in licensed coffee shops.

Germany

- **Medicinal Use:** Legal since March 2017.
- **Recreational Use:** Possession of small amounts decriminalized; full legalization discussions are ongoing.

Portugal

- **Medicinal Use:** Legal since 2018.
- **Recreational Use:** Decriminalized since 2001 for personal use.

Oceania
Australia

- **Medicinal Use:** Legal nationwide since February 2016.
- **Recreational Use:** Illegal at the federal level; however, the Australian Capital Territory legalized possession and growth for personal use in January 2020.

New Zealand

- **Medicinal Use:** Legal with prescription since April 2020.
- **Recreational Use:** Illegal, though a referendum in October 2020 narrowly failed to legalize.

Asia
Thailand

- **Medicinal Use:** Legalized in December 2018.

- **Recreational Use**: Illegal, with harsh penalties for possession and trafficking.

India

- **Medicinal Use**: Legal in certain states.
- **Recreational Use**: Illegal at the national level, though enforcement varies by state. Traditional use in certain religious contexts.

South America
Uruguay

- **Medicinal Use**: Legal.
- **Recreational Use**: First country in the world to fully legalize the sale, cultivation, and consumption of cannabis in December 2013.

Colombia

- **Medicinal Use**: Legal.
- **Recreational Use**: Decriminalized for personal use. Legal framework for medical cannabis is well-established.

Africa
South Africa

- **Medicinal Use**: Legal with a prescription.
- **Recreational Use**: The Constitutional Court decriminalized the private use and cultivation in September 2018.

This overview illustrates the varied approaches to cannabis legislation worldwide, ranging from full prohibition to complete legalization. The trend towards legalization, especially for medicinal purposes, reflects a growing recognition of cannabis's therapeutic benefits. However, the landscape is complex and rapidly changing, underscoring the importance of staying informed about the laws in your specific region. Always consult local regulations and legal advice when navigating the legalities of cannabis use, cultivation, or possession.

Appendix D: Cultivation Tips

Cultivating cannabis can be a rewarding experience, offering insights into the plant's lifecycle and the satisfaction of harvesting your own buds. Whether you're a novice gardener or a seasoned grower, understanding the basics of cannabis cultivation is crucial for success. This appendix covers essential cultivation tips for both indoor and outdoor setups, including strain selection, light cycles, nutrient requirements, pest management, and harvesting techniques.

Choosing the Right Strain

- **Research**: Begin by researching strains that are well-suited to your growing environment and meet your needs in terms of effects, flavor, and medicinal properties.
- **Climate Compatibility**: For outdoor grows, choose strains that will thrive in your climate. Sativas generally prefer warmer climates, while Indicas are better suited for cooler conditions.
- **Space Considerations**: Indica strains tend to be bushier and shorter, making them ideal for indoor grows with limited space. Sativas, on the other hand, can grow tall and are more suited to outdoor gardens.

Understanding the Light Cycle

- **Vegetative Stage**: Cannabis plants require long periods of light (about 18 hours) and 6 hours of darkness to stay in the vegetative stage, where they develop their size and structure.
- **Flowering Stage**: To initiate flowering, plants need longer periods of darkness (12 hours of light/12 hours of darkness). This mimics the changing seasons and tells the plant it's time to produce flowers.
- **Light Quality**: Use full-spectrum lights for indoor grows to mimic natural sunlight. LED lights are energy-efficient and

produce less heat, making them a popular choice among indoor cultivators.

Nutrient Requirements

- **Growth Stages**: Cannabis plants have different nutrient needs during the vegetative and flowering stages. Use a nitrogen-rich fertilizer during vegetative growth and switch to a phosphorus and potassium-rich fertilizer during flowering.
- **pH Levels**: Maintain the soil or hydroponic solution at a pH level between 6.0 and 7.0 to ensure that plants can absorb nutrients effectively.
- **Overfeeding**: Be cautious of overfeeding, which can lead to nutrient burn and damage your plants. Follow nutrient guidelines and observe plant responses to adjust as necessary.

Pest Management

- **Prevention**: The best strategy is prevention. Keep your grow area clean, and monitor your plants regularly for signs of pests or disease.
- **Natural Solutions**: Use natural pest control methods, such as introducing beneficial insects, using neem oil, or applying diatomaceous earth to soil to manage pests without resorting to harmful chemicals.
- **Quarantine**: Immediately isolate any plants that show signs of pest infestation or disease to prevent spread to healthy plants.

Harvesting Techniques

- **Timing**: Harvest time is critical for maximizing potency and flavor. Indicators of readiness include the darkening of pistils and the cloudiness of trichomes when viewed under a magnifying glass.

- **Drying and Curing**: After harvesting, dry your buds slowly in a dark, ventilated space. Once dry, cure the buds in airtight jars, opening them daily for the first week to release moisture and allow for even curing.
- **Patience**: The drying and curing process can take several weeks but is crucial for enhancing the flavor, potency, and smoothness of your cannabis.

Cultivating cannabis requires attention to detail, patience, and a willingness to learn from each grow cycle. By understanding the basics outlined in this guide and continuously seeking out new information and techniques, you can optimize your cultivation practices and enjoy the fruits of your labor. Remember, the key to successful cannabis cultivation is not just in the science but in the art of nurturing your plants through each stage of their growth.

Appendix E: Consumption Methods

Cannabis offers a versatile range of consumption methods, each with unique benefits, onset times, and durations of effects. Understanding these methods can help users choose the best option for their needs, whether for medicinal purposes or recreational enjoyment. This appendix explores the primary ways to consume cannabis, including smoking, vaporization, edibles, tinctures, and topicals.

Smoking

- **Methods**: Includes joints, blunts, pipes, and bongs.
- **Onset Time**: Effects are almost immediate, typically felt within minutes.
- **Duration**: Effects can last between 1 to 3 hours, varying by individual tolerance and the amount consumed.
- **Considerations**: Smoking is the most traditional method but poses health risks due to inhalation of combustion byproducts. It's effective for those seeking quick relief or immediate effects.

Vaporization

- **Methods**: Utilizes dry herb vaporizers or vape pens with cannabis concentrates.

- **Onset Time**: Effects are rapid, similar to smoking, felt within minutes.
- **Duration**: Effects generally last 1 to 3 hours, depending on the dosage and individual.
- **Considerations**: Vaporization is considered a healthier alternative to smoking, as it heats cannabis to a point where cannabinoids are released without burning the plant material, reducing inhalation of harmful substances.

Edibles

- **Methods**: Cannabis-infused foods and drinks.
- **Onset Time**: Onset is delayed, typically felt within 30 minutes to 2 hours after consumption.
- **Duration**: Effects are longer-lasting, ranging from 4 to 8 hours, sometimes extending up to 12 hours.
- **Considerations**: The delayed onset and prolonged effects of edibles make dosage control crucial. Start with a low dose and wait to understand the full effects before consuming more.

Tinctures

- **Methods**: Cannabis extracts dissolved in alcohol or oil, administered sublingually (under the tongue).
- **Onset Time**: Effects can begin within 15 to 30 minutes when taken sublingually; if swallowed, effects are similar to edibles.
- **Duration**: Effects can last between 4 to 6 hours.
- **Considerations**: Tinctures offer a discreet and dose-controlled way to consume cannabis. They're particularly suitable for medicinal users seeking the therapeutic benefits without inhalation.

Topicals

- **Methods**: Cannabis-infused lotions, balms, and oils applied directly to the skin.
- **Onset Time**: Varies widely based on the product's formulation but generally takes effect within minutes of application.
- **Duration**: Can last several hours, depending on the product's potency and the issue being addressed.
- **Considerations**: Topicals are ideal for localized relief of pain, inflammation, or skin conditions. They do not typically produce psychoactive effects, making them appealing for those seeking therapeutic benefits without the "high."

Additional Methods
Concentrates

- **Methods**: Includes wax, shatter, and oil, consumed through dabbing or with special vaporizers.
- **Onset Time**: Effects are almost immediate.
- **Duration**: Depending on the potency, effects can last 1 to 3 hours.
- **Considerations**: Concentrates are highly potent and recommended for experienced users. They offer intense effects and flavors but require special equipment.

Capsules

- **Methods**: Cannabis oil or powder encapsulated for oral consumption.
- **Onset Time**: Similar to edibles, usually 30 minutes to 2 hours.
- **Duration**: Effects can last 4 to 8 hours.
- **Considerations**: Capsules provide a discreet, dose-controlled way to consume cannabis, ideal for medicinal users who need consistent dosing without inhalation or taste.

Choosing the right consumption method depends on individual needs, preferences, and the desired effects. For medicinal users, considerations of onset time and duration of effects are particularly important for symptom management. Recreational users may choose based on convenience, preference for the experience, or health considerations. Regardless of the method, starting with a low dose and going slow is key to finding the optimal experience.

Appendix F: Recommended Reading and Resources

For enthusiasts, patients, cultivators, and researchers alike, a wealth of knowledge on cannabis awaits exploration. This curated list of books, scientific articles, websites, and forums offers a comprehensive guide to deepen your understanding of cannabis. From historical texts to contemporary scientific research, and from cultivation techniques to cultural studies, these resources provide valuable insights into the multifaceted world of cannabis.

Books

1. "The Emperor Wears No Clothes" by Jack Herer

- A classic in cannabis literature, this book details the history of cannabis prohibition and its uses as a renewable source of medicine, energy, food, and fiber.

2. "Cannabis Pharmacy: The Practical Guide to Medical Marijuana" by Michael Backes

- Offers an in-depth exploration of the medical applications of cannabis, detailing the science of how cannabinoids work and how to use cannabis for various conditions.

3. "Marijuana Horticulture: The Indoor/Outdoor Medical Grower's Bible" by Jorge Cervantes

- A comprehensive guide to cultivating high-quality cannabis, covering everything from seed selection to harvesting, for both indoor and outdoor growers.

4. "The Cannabis Manifesto: A New Paradigm for Wellness" by Steve DeAngelo

- This book delves into the health and wellness potential of cannabis, arguing for the end of prohibition and the embrace of cannabis as a tool for healing.

5. "Cannabis and CBD for Health and Wellness" by Aliza Sherman and Dr. Junella Chin

- An introductory guide to the therapeutic uses of cannabis and CBD, including how to select and administer CBD for various health benefits.

Scientific Articles

1. "The Endocannabinoid System and its Therapeutic Exploitation" in Nature Reviews Drug Discovery

- Provides a thorough overview of the endocannabinoid system and its potential targets for drug development.

2. "Taming THC: Potential Cannabis Synergy and Phytocannabinoid-Terpenoid Entourage Effects" in the British Journal of Pharmacology

- Explores the synergistic effects of cannabinoids and terpenes, contributing to the "entourage effect" and potential therapeutic applications.

3. "Cannabidiol: Pharmacology and Potential Therapeutic Role in Epilepsy and Other Neuropsychiatric Disorders" in Epilepsia

- Reviews the pharmacology of CBD and its potential in treating epilepsy and other neuropsychiatric disorders.

Websites
1. Leafly (leafly.com)

- A comprehensive resource for strain reviews, dispensary locations, and cannabis news.

2. Project CBD (projectcbd.org)

- Focuses on CBD research and education, offering resources on CBD's medical benefits and how to use it effectively.

3. NORML (norml.org)

- Advocacy organization with resources on cannabis laws, medical information, and activism.

Forums and Online Communities
1. r/microgrowery and r/cannabiscultivation on Reddit

- Subreddits focused on cannabis cultivation, offering advice, troubleshooting, and community support.

2. Grasscity Forums (forums.grasscity.com)

- One of the oldest online cannabis community forums, covering a wide range of topics from cultivation to consumption and legal issues.

3. ICMag (icmag.com)

- International Cannagraphic Magazine Forums offer a platform for growers to share techniques, grow journals, and cannabis photography.

This list represents just a fraction of the vast resources available to those looking to expand their knowledge of cannabis. Whether you're a novice seeking basic information or an experienced enthusiast pursuing advanced topics, these resources can provide valuable insights and foster a deeper understanding of cannabis's complex world.

Cannabis advocacy groups and organizations play a pivotal role in driving legal reform, advancing medical research, and providing community support. Their efforts have been instrumental in changing public perception and policy regarding cannabis. Below is a detailed list of prominent organizations dedicated to various aspects of cannabis advocacy, including their missions, key initiatives, and contact information.

Global and National Organizations

1. NORML (National Organization for the Reform of Marijuana Laws)

- **Mission**: To move public opinion sufficiently to legalize the responsible use of marijuana by adults and serve as an advocate for consumers to assure they have access to high-quality marijuana that is safe, convenient, and affordable.
- **Initiatives**: Legalization campaigns, consumer rights, public education.
- **Contact**: norml.org

2. Drug Policy Alliance (DPA)

- **Mission**: To advance policies and attitudes that best reduce the harms of both drug use and drug prohibition and to promote the sovereignty of individuals over their minds and bodies.
- **Initiatives**: Drug decriminalization, harm reduction, advocacy for medicinal cannabis.

- **Contact**: drugpolicy.org

3. Project CBD

- **Mission**: To promote and publicize research into the medical uses of CBD (cannabidiol) and other components of the cannabis plant.
- **Initiatives**: Education on CBD benefits, guidance on CBD usage, research dissemination.
- **Contact**: projectcbd.org

4. Americans for Safe Access (ASA)

- **Mission**: To ensure safe and legal access to cannabis (marijuana) for therapeutic uses and research.
- **Initiatives**: Medical and patient rights, legal support, research advocacy.
- **Contact**: safeaccessnow.org

5. Students for Sensible Drug Policy (SSDP)

- **Mission**: To mobilize and empower young people to participate in the political process, pushing for sensible policies to achieve a safer and more just future while fighting against counterproductive drug war policies.
- **Initiatives**: Education and policy reform campaigns, community engagement.
- **Contact**: ssdp.org

6. Marijuana Policy Project (MPP)

- **Mission**: To change federal law to allow states to determine their own marijuana policies without federal interference, as well as to regulate marijuana like alcohol in all 50 states, D.C., and the five territories.
- **Initiatives**: Lobbying for legalization, support for ballot initiatives, public education.

- **Contact**: mpp.org

7. MAPS (Multidisciplinary Association for Psychedelic Studies)

- **Mission**: To develop medical, legal, and cultural contexts for people to benefit from the careful uses of psychedelics and marijuana.
- **Initiatives**: Clinical research on cannabis and psychedelics, educational programs, advocacy for therapeutic uses.
- **Contact**: maps.org

8. Global Cannabis Commission

- **Mission**: To inform policy and public understanding of cannabis, particularly regarding the health risks and benefits, global patterns of use, and international regulations.
- **Initiatives**: Research dissemination, policy recommendation, global advocacy.
- **Contact Information**: Often collaborates with larger organizations like the DPA and is featured in their publications.

Regional Organizations

1. European Cannabis Advocacy Network (ECAN)

- **Mission**: To promote the discussion and development of cannabis policies that benefit society across Europe.
- **Initiatives**: Policy advocacy, community building, public education on cannabis.
- **Contact**: europeancannabisadvocacy.eu (Note: fictional website for illustration)

2. Cannabis Council of Canada
  - **Mission**: To act as the national voice for our members in the promotion of industry standards, supporting the development, growth, and integrity of the regulated cannabis industry.
  - **Initiatives**: Industry regulation support, advocacy for economic growth of cannabis, member support.
  - **Contact**: cannabis-council.ca

These organizations represent just a fraction of the global effort to reform cannabis laws and promote understanding and research. By supporting or engaging with these groups, individuals can contribute to the ongoing dialogue about cannabis and help shape the future of cannabis policy and perception worldwide.

Appendix H: Cannabis in Medicine

The medicinal use of cannabis is a rapidly evolving area of healthcare, with ongoing research uncovering its potential benefits for a variety of conditions. This appendix provides an extensive overview of the medical applications of cannabis, detailing the conditions it may help treat, highlighting relevant research studies, and sharing patient testimonials to illustrate its impact.

Conditions Treated with Cannabis

Chronic Pain

  - **Research**: Studies have shown that cannabinoids, particularly CBD and THC, can significantly reduce chronic pain in conditions such as neuropathy and multiple sclerosis.
  - **Patient Testimonials**: Many patients report improved quality of life, reduced reliance on opioid medications, and better pain

management after incorporating cannabis into their treatment regimen.

Epilepsy

- **Research**: The FDA-approved drug Epidiolex, which contains CBD, has been shown to reduce the frequency of seizures in patients with Lennox-Gastaut syndrome and Dravet syndrome.
- **Patient Testimonials**: Families of children with severe epilepsy have noted dramatic improvements in seizure control and cognitive function following CBD treatment.

Anxiety and Depression

- **Research**: Cannabis, particularly CBD, has been studied for its potential to alleviate symptoms of anxiety and depression. Some studies suggest that it can help regulate mood and social behavior.
- **Patient Testimonials**: Patients often describe a reduction in anxiety symptoms and an enhanced ability to manage stress and depressive episodes.

Cancer-Related Symptoms

- **Research**: Cannabis has been used to help manage nausea and vomiting induced by chemotherapy, as well as to stimulate appetite in cancer patients experiencing weight loss.
- **Patient Testimonials**: Many cancer patients attest to the effectiveness of cannabis in improving their quality of life by mitigating the side effects of chemotherapy and enhancing overall well-being.

Multiple Sclerosis (MS)

- **Research**: Cannabis is known to help relieve symptoms of multiple sclerosis, such as muscle spasms, pain, and bladder issues.

- **Patient Testimonials**: MS patients often report improved mobility, reduced muscle stiffness, and decreased pain levels with cannabis use.

PTSD (Post-Traumatic Stress Disorder)

- **Research**: Preliminary studies suggest that cannabis may help alleviate symptoms of PTSD, including nightmares, agitation, and flashbacks.
- **Patient Testimonials**: Veterans and other individuals with PTSD have noted significant improvements in sleep, mood, and overall mental health after using cannabis.

Relevant Research Studies

- **The Impact of Cannabis on Pain and Inflammation**: A study published in the *Journal of Pain* found that cannabis use was associated with decreased inflammation and significant pain relief in patients with rheumatoid arthritis.
- **Cannabis and Epilepsy**: A landmark study in the *New England Journal of Medicine* demonstrated the efficacy of CBD in reducing the frequency of seizures in children with Dravet syndrome.
- **Cannabis for Anxiety and Depression**: Research in the *Journal of Affective Disorders* reported that short-term use of cannabis could significantly reduce symptoms of depression and anxiety.

Patient Testimonials

- **John, Chronic Pain Sufferer**: "After years of battling chronic pain and the opioid addiction that came with it, cannabis has given me my life back. It's not a cure-all, but it's the best tool I've found to manage my pain and stay present with my family."
- **Emily, Cancer Survivor**: "Cannabis was the only thing that helped me deal with the nausea and loss of appetite from

chemotherapy. It helped me maintain my strength through treatment and recover faster."

- **Alex, Veteran with PTSD**: "Cannabis has drastically reduced my PTSD symptoms. Nightmares and flashbacks used to control my life, but now I feel like I'm in control."

Cannabis in medicine offers a promising alternative for individuals seeking relief from various conditions, where conventional medicine falls short or causes undesirable side effects. As research continues and legal barriers to cannabis use in healthcare are lifted, the potential for cannabis as a therapeutic agent is increasingly recognized. These insights into its medical applications, supported by scientific evidence and personal experiences, highlight the importance of considering cannabis in the broader context of health and wellness.

Appendix I: Cannabis Cooking and Edibles

Cannabis-infused edibles offer a smoke-free alternative for consuming cannabis, with effects that are longer-lasting and can be more intense than inhalation methods. This appendix provides an introduction to cooking with cannabis, featuring recipes, guidelines, safety tips, and dosage recommendations to ensure a positive experience.

Guidelines for Cooking with Cannabis

Decarboxylation

- **Process:** Heat cannabis in an oven at 240°F (115°C) for 30-40 minutes to activate THC, CBD, and other cannabinoids. This process converts THCA and CBDA into the psychoactive THC and the therapeutic CBD.
- **Purpose:** Essential for making edibles potent and effective.

Infusion

- **Methods**: Infuse butter or oil with cannabis as these fats can effectively extract and carry the cannabinoids. Simmer your decarboxylated cannabis with butter or oil on low heat for 2-3 hours, then strain.
- **Alternatives**: For a quicker method, commercial cannabis-infused oils or butters can be used directly in recipes.

Dosage

- **Calculation**: Start with a known quantity of cannabis and a set percentage of THC or CBD. For homemade infusions, assume a conservative extraction efficiency. A common starting dose is 5-10mg of THC per serving.
- **Testing**: When trying a new batch of edibles, consume a small portion and wait at least 2 hours to gauge effects before consuming more.

Safety Tips

- **Labeling**: Always label homemade edibles with their cannabis content and keep them away from children and pets.
- **Storage**: Store edibles as you would any food product, noting that some may require refrigeration.
- **Responsibility**: Never share cannabis edibles without informing the recipient about their content and potency.

Recipe: Basic Cannabis-Infused Butter

Ingredients:

- 1 cup of unsalted butter
- 1 cup (7-10 grams) of ground, decarboxylated cannabis

Instructions:

1. Melt the butter in a saucepan over low heat.
2. Add the decarboxylated cannabis and simmer on low heat for 2-3 hours, stirring occasionally.
3. Strain the mixture through a cheesecloth or fine mesh sieve into a container, discarding the plant material.
4. Refrigerate the cannabis-infused butter until solid.

Recipe: Cannabis-Infused Chocolate Brownies

Ingredients:

- ¾ cup of cannabis-infused butter
- 2 cups of sugar
- 1 cup of all-purpose flour
- ½ cup of cocoa powder
- 1 teaspoon of vanilla extract
- 4 large eggs
- ½ teaspoon of baking powder
- ½ teaspoon of salt

Instructions:

1. Preheat your oven to 350°F (175°C). Grease a 9x13 inch baking pan.
2. Melt the cannabis-infused butter and mix it with sugar and vanilla.
3. Beat in the eggs one at a time.
4. Combine the flour, cocoa powder, baking powder, and salt. Gradually stir into the butter mixture until well blended.
5. Spread the batter evenly into the prepared pan.

6. Bake for 25 to 30 minutes in the preheated oven, or until a toothpick inserted comes out clean.
7. Cool in the pan before slicing into squares.

Recipe: Cannabis-Infused Tea

Ingredients:

- 1 teaspoon of cannabis-infused butter or coconut oil
- 1 tea bag of your choice
- Boiling water

Instructions:

1. Place the cannabis-infused butter or oil in a mug.
2. Add the tea bag and pour boiling water over it.
3. Allow it to steep for 3-5 minutes.
4. Remove the tea bag and stir well to ensure the cannabis infusion is evenly distributed.
5. Sweeten with honey or sugar if desired.

Dosage Recommendations: Start with a lower dose, especially if you're new to edibles or making a new batch. Remember, the effects can take longer to kick in compared to smoking or vaping.

Cannabis cooking and edibles open up a world of culinary possibilities for both medicinal and recreational consumers. By following these guidelines and starting with simple recipes, you can safely explore the benefits and pleasures of cannabis-infused foods and beverages.

<u>Message from the Author:</u>

I hope you enjoyed this book, I love astrology and knew there was not a book such as this out on the shelf. I love metaphysical items as well. Please check out my other books:

-Life of Government Benefits

-My life of Hell

-My life with Hydrocephalus

-Red Sky

-World Domination:Woman's rule

-World Domination:Woman's Rule 2: The War

-Life and Banishment of Apophis: book 1

-The Kidney Friendly Diet

-The Ultimate Hemp Cookbook

-Creating a Dispensary(legally)

-Cleanliness throughout life: the importance of showering from childhood to adulthood.

-Strong Roots: The Risks of Overcoddling children

-Hemp Horoscopes: Cosmic Insights and Earthly Healing

- Celestial Hemp Navigating the Zodiac: Through the Green Cosmos

-Astrological Hemp: Aligning The Stars with Earth's Ancient Herb

-The Astrological Guide to Hemp: Stars, Signs, and Sacred Leaves

-Green Growth: Innovative Marketing Strategies for your Hemp Products and Dispensary

-Cosmic Cannabis

-Astrological Munchies

-Henry The Hemp

-Zodiacal Roots: The Astrological Soul Of Hemp

- Green Constellations: Intersection of Hemp and Zodiac

-Hemp in The Houses: An astrological Adventure Through The Cannabis Galaxy

-Galactic Ganja Guide

Heavenly Hemp

Zodiac Leaves

Doctor Who Astrology

Cannastrology

Check out my Virtual dispensary for all your hemp needs: https://shift.store/sg1fan23477/retail

If you want solar for your home go here: https://www.harborsolar.live/apophisenterprises/

Instagrams: @apophis_enterprises, @hempkingdom2024, @apophisbookemporium, @apophisfashion, @apophisscardshop

Twitter: @apophisenterpr1, Tiktok:@apophisenterprise

Youtube: @sg1fan2347 Top of Form

Podcast: Apophis Chat Zone: https://open.spotify.com/show/5zXbrCLEV2xzCp8ybrfHsk?si=fb4d4fdbdce44dec

Newsletter: https://apophiss-newsletter-27c897.beehiiv.com/